ROYAL COURT

Royal Court Theatre presents

FORTY WINKS

by **Kevin Elyot**

First performance at the Royal Court Jerwood Theatre Downstairs,
Sloane Square, London on 28 October 2004.

FORTY WINKS

by **Kevin Elyot**

Cast
Diana **Anastasia Hille**
Danny **Stephen Kennedy**
Hermia/Celia **Carey Mulligan**
Charlie **Paul Ready**
Don **Dominic Rowan**
Howard **Simon Wilson**

Director **Katie Mitchell**
Designer **Hildegard Bechtler**
Costume Designer **Iona Kenrick**
Lighting Designer **Paule Constable**
Sound Designer **Gareth Fry**
Associate Sound Designer **Carolyn Downing**
Assistant Designer **Luke Smith**
Casting **Sam Jones**
Production Manager **Paul Handley**
Stage Manager **Tariq Rifaat**
Deputy Stage Manager **Pippa Meyer**
Assistant Stage Manager **Sally Higson**
Costume Supervisor **Jemimah Tomlinson**
Company Voice Work **Patsy Rodenburg**
Set built by **Miraculous Engineering**
Set painted by **Charlotte Gainey**

The Royal Court would like to thank the following for their help with this production: International Shakespeare Globe

THE COMPANY

Kevin Elyot (writer)
For the Royal Court: Mouth to Mouth (& West End), My Night with Reg (& West End).
Other theatre includes: The Day I Stood Still (National), Artists and Admirers (new translation, RSC); Coming Clean (Bush).
Screenplays include: Killing Time, The Moonstone, My Night with Reg, No Night is Too Long, Five Little Pigs, Death on the Nile, The Body in the Library.
Awards include the Samuel Beckett Award for Coming Clean, the Evening Standard, Laurence Olivier, Writers' Guild and Critics' Circle Awards for My Night with Reg, and the Writers' Guild Award for Killing Time.

Hildegard Bechtler (designer)
For the Royal Court: The Sweetest Swing in Baseball, Blood, Terrorism, Blasted, The Changing Room.
Other theatre includes: The Goat or Who is Sylvia? (Almeida); The Master Builder (Albery); Iphigenia at Aulis, The Merchant of Venice, Richard II, King Lear (RNT); La Maison de Poupée (Theatre de l'Europe, Paris); Footfalls (Garrick); The St. Pancras Project (LIFT); Electra (RSC/Riverside/Bobigny, Paris); Hedda Gabler (Abbey, Dublin/Playhouse, London); Coriolanus (Salzburg Festival).
Opera includes: The Ring Cycle, Das Rheingold, Walküre, Siegfried and Götterdämmerung (Scottish Opera/Edinburgh Festival); Lady Macbeth of Mtsensk (Sydney Opera House); Paul Bunyan (ROH); War and Peace, Boris Gudonov, Peter Grimes, Lohengrin, The Bacchae (ENO); Les Dialogues des Carmelites (Japan/Paris Opera); Simon Boccanegra, Peter Grimes (Staatsoper, Munich); Don Carlos, Wozzeck, Katya Kabanova (Opera North); Don Giovanni (Glyndebourne); La Wally (Bregenz Festival/Amsterdam Musik Theatre).
Film and television includes: The Merchant of Venice, Richard II, The Wasteland, Hedda Gabler, Coming Up Roses, Business as Usual.

Paule Constable (lighting designer)
For the Royal Court: Nightsongs, Boy Gets Girl, Mountain Language/Ashes to Ashes, Presence, Credible Witness, The Country, Dublin Carol, The Weir, The Glory of Living.
Other theatre includes: The Prince of Homburg, The Seagull, Tales from Ovid, The Dispute, Uncle Vanya, Beckett Shorts, The Mysteries (RSC); Ivanov, Jumpers, Three Sisters, His Dark Materials, Play Without Words, The Villain's Opera, Darker Face of the Earth, Haroun and the Sea of Stories, Caucasian Chalk Circle (RNT); Proof, Little Foxes (Donmar); Don Carlos (Sheffield Crucible); Amadeus (West End, Broadway); Vagina Monologues (West End); The Servant, Pericles, Oliver Twist (Lyric); More Grimms' Tales (Young Vic & New York);

four productions for Theatre de Complicite.
Opera includes: the Royal Opera House, English National Opera, Welsh National Opera, Scottish Opera, Opera North, Glyndebourne.

Carolyn Downing (associate sound designer)
Theatre includes: Habitats, Under the Curse (Gate) A Doll's House, The Double Bass, The Provok'd Wife, Mongoose (Southwark Playhouse); Macbeth (Out of Joint); Gone to Earth (Shared Experience); Waiting for the Parade (Mountview); Moonshed (Royal Exchange); The Watery Part of the World (Sound & Fury); Heavenly Hades (Red Circle); Small World (Sue Lee and Kosta Andreas).

Gareth Fry (sound designer)
For the Royal Court: Under the Whaleback, Nightsongs, Face to the Wall, Genoa 01 (with Complicite), Redundant, Mountain Language, Ashes to Ashes, The Country, Holy Mothers.
Other theatre includes: Iphigenia at Aulis, Three Sisters, Ivanov, The Oresteia (RNT); Strange Poetry Noise of Time, Mnemonic (Complicite); World Music, The Dark (Donmar); Zero Degrees and Drifting (Unlimited); Macbeth (Out of Joint); Galileo's Daughter, Don Juan, Man & Superman, Blithe Spirit (Peter Hall season, Theatre Royal Bath; Time & Space (Living Dance Studio, Beijing); Shape of Metal (Abbey, Dublin); Living Costs (DV8 at Tate Modern); The Watery Part of the World, States of Shock (BAC); Midsummer Night's Dream (Regent's Park); Eccentricities of a Nightingale (Gate, Dublin) Mr. Placebo (Traverse); Forbidden Broadway (Albery); Accrington Pals (Chichester); Wexford Trilogy (OSC); Play to Win (Yellow Earth); Snow Queen, The Last Yellow, Makropulos Secret (Chelsea); Showstopper, Brothers of the Brush, Two Boys in Bed on a Cold Winter's Morning (Arts); It Took More Than One Man, The Rivals (Southwark); Something About Us (Lyric).

Anastasia Hille
For the Royal Court: Ashes to Ashes/Mountain Language (& Lincoln Center, New York).
Other theatre includes: The Dark, Morphic Resonance (Donmar); The Winter's Tale (RSC); The Oresteia, Marat Sade, Macbeth, Richard III (RNT) The Maids (RSC/Young Vic); Mad World My Masters, Two Gentlemen of Verona (Globe); As You Like It (Globe & Tokyo); Uncle Vanya, Therese Raqu (Young Vic); The Cenci (Almeida); The Duchess of Malfi, Measure for Measure (Cheek By Jowl); Three Tall Women (Wyndham's); Arms and the Ma (Cambridge Theatre Co); James MacMillan's Parthenogenesis (Edinburgh Festival).
Television includes: Red Dwarf, Jeeves and Wooste Kavanagh QC, Eleven Men Against Eleven, Harvest Moon, Trial and Retribution, Dance to the Music of

Time, Big Women, Storm Damage, RK0 281, The
Cazalets, Outside the Rules, Cutting It.
Film includes: The Wisdom of Crocodiles,
The Escort, New Year's Day, Five Seconds to Spare,
The Hole.
Radio includes: Strangers and Brothers,
The Heiligenstadt Summer, Hippomania, Who's
Afraid of Virginia Woolf?, The Pallisers.

Stephen Kennedy

For the Royal Court: Loyal Women, The Force of
Change.
Other theatre includes: Popcorn (Liverpool
Playhouse); Comedians, The Contractor (Oxford
Stage Co.); Juno and The Paycock (Donmar);
Measure For Measure, Shadows - Riders To The Sea
& The Shadow Of The Glen, This Lime Tree Bower,
Macbeth (RSC); Translations (Royal Lyceum,
Edinburgh); Phaedra (Gate, Dublin); Double Helix
(Peacock, Dublin); Miss Julie (Andrew's Lane);
Macbeth (Kilkenny Castle); The Taming Of The
Shrew (Lyric, Belfast); Belfry (Druid); Hamlet,
The Honey Spike (Abbey, Dublin); On The Outside,
Silverlands, Gadai Gear na Geamh Oiche (Peacock,
Dublin).
Television includes: The Hanging Gale, The Snapper,
Parents Night, Making Waves, The Vice.
Film includes: Braveheart, The Snapper.

Carey Mulligan

Theatre includes: Tower Block Dreams (Riverside);
Once Upon a Mattress (Elgiva, Chesham); Rites
(Millennium Centre, Woldingham); Sweet Charity,
Tongues of Flame (Woldingham).
Film includes: Pride and Prejudice.

Katie Mitchell (director)

For the Royal Court: Face To The Wall, Nightsongs,
Mountain Language/Ashes to Ashes, The Country,
Live Like Pigs.
Other theatre includes: Arden of Faversham
(Old Red Lion); Vassa Zheleznova, Women of Troy,
The House of Bernarda Alba (Gate); A Woman
Killed with Kindness, The Dybbuk, Henry VI, Easter,
The Phoenician Women, The Mysteries, Beckett
Shorts, Uncle Vanya (RSC); Three Sisters, Rutherford
and Son, The Machine Wreckers, The Oresteia, Three
Sisters, Iphigenia at Aulis (RNT); The Last One,
Iphigenia at Aulis (Abbey, Dublin); Endgame
(Donmar); Attempts On Her Life (Piccolo Theatre,
Milan).
Opera includes: Don Giovanni, Jenufa and Katya
Kabanova, Jephta (Welsh National Opera).
Awards include: 1996 Evening Standard Award for
Best Director for The Phoenician Women.
Katie is an Associate Director at the National.

Paul Ready

For the Royal Court: Terrorism, Black Milk,
Crazyblackmuthafuckin'self.
Other theatre includes: World Music (Donmar &
Sheffield Crucible); Comedy of Errors (Bristol Old
Vic & New Vic); Romeo and Juliet
(Liverpool Playhouse); Mother Clapp's Molly House
(RNT, Aldwych & National Studio); Twelfth Night
(Liverpool Playhouse & Everyman); Cuckoos (Gate &
National Studio); The Beggar's Opera (Broomhill
Opera/Wilton's Music Hall).
Television includes: Spine Chillers, Born and Bred,
Blackpool, Life Begins, Jeffrey Archer - The Truth,
Heartbeat, Tipping the Velvet, Chambers, Harry
Enfield Presents, Princess, Plain Jane, Doctors.
Film includes: Maybe Baby, Angels & Insects.
Radio includes: The Girl From The Sea.

Dominic Rowan

Theatre includes: Iphigenia at Aulis, Mourning
Becomes Electra, Three Sisters, The Talking Cure,
Private Lives (RNT); Lobby Hero (Donmar/New
Ambassadors); Merchant of Venice, Two Gentlemen
of Verona, Talk Of The City (RSC); Sexual Perversity
in Chicago (Crucible, Sheffield); Look Back In Anger,
The Rivals, Charlie's Aunt (Manchester); Playhouse
Creatures (Old Vic); Talk of the City (Young Vic);
A Collier's Friday Night (Hampstead).
Television includes: North Square, A Rather English
Marriage, Between the Lines, Devil's Advocate, No
Bananas, Emma, Swallow, Rescue Me, Lost World,
Hearts and Bones, The Tenant of Wildfell Hall, Silent
Witness (srs VI), Holby City, Celeb, Doc Martin.
Film includes: David, Tulse Lupers' Suitcases, Pressure
Points.
Radio includes: Talk of the City, Mill on the Floss.

Luke Smith (assistant designer)

For the Royal Court: The Sweetest Swing in Baseball,
Terrorism.
Other theatre includes: The Goat or Who is Sylvia?
(Almeida); The Master Builder (Albery); Iphigenia at
Aulis, Primo (RNT).
Opera includes:
Gotterdammerung (Scottish Opera/Edinburgh
Festival).
Film includes: The Dance of Shiva, Ghosthunter.

Simon Wilson

Theatre includes: Gone to Earth (Shared
Experience); Abigail's Party (Hampstead & tour);
Barbarians, Donkeys' Years (Salisbury Playhouse);
Rosencrantz & Guildernstern are Dead (West
Yorkshire Playhouse), Taming of the Shrew
(Jardin Shakespeare, Paris).
Television includes: Inspector Lynley Mysteries,
Auf Wiedersehen Pet, A Thing Called Love, Murphy's
Law, Hear The Silence, Wire in the Blood.
Film includes: Woman X.

THE ENGLISH STAGE COMPANY AT THE ROYAL COURT

The English Stage Company at the Royal Court opened in 1956 as a subsidised theatre producing new British plays, international plays and some classical revivals.

The first artistic director George Devine aimed to create a writers' theatre, 'a place where the dramatist is acknowledged as the fundamental creative force in the theatre and where the play is more important than the actors, the director, the designer'. The urgent need was to find a contemporary style in which the play, the acting, direction and design are all combined. He believed that 'the battle will be a long one to continue to create the right conditions for writers to work in'.

Devine aimed to discover 'hard-hitting, uncompromising writers whose plays are stimulating, provocative and exciting'. The Royal Court production of John Osborne's Look Back in Anger in May 1956 is now seen as the decisive starting point of modern British drama and the policy created a new generation of British playwrights. The first wave included John Osborne, Arnold Wesker, John Arden, Ann Jellicoe, N F Simpson and Edward Bond. Early seasons included new international plays by Bertolt Brecht, Eugène Ionesco, Samuel Beckett, Jean-Paul Sartre and Marguerite Duras.

The theatre started with the 400-seat proscenium arch Theatre Downstairs, and in 1969 opened a second theatre, the 60-seat studio Theatre Upstairs. Some productions transfer to the West End, such as Terry Johnson's Hitchcock Blonde, Caryl Churchill's Far Away and Conor McPherson's The Weir. Recent touring productions include Sarah Kane's 4.48 Psychosis (US tour) and Ché Walker's Flesh Wound (Galway Arts Festival). The Royal Court also co-produces plays which have transferred to the West End or toured internationally, such as Conor McPherson's Shining City (with Gate Theatre, Dublin), Sebastian Barry's The Steward of Christendom and Mark Ravenhill's Shopping and Fucking (with Out of Joint), Martin McDonagh's The Beauty Queen Of Leenane (with Druid Theatre Company), Ayub Khan Din's East is East (with Tamasha Theatre Company).

Since 1994 the Royal Court's artistic policy has again been vigorously directed to finding and producing a new generation of playwrights. The writers include Joe Penhall, Rebecca Prichard, Michael Wynne, Nick Grosso, Judy Upton, Meredith Oakes, Sarah Kane, Anthony Neilson, Judith Johnson, James Stock, Jez Butterworth,

photo: Andy Chopping

Marina Carr, Phyllis Nagy, Simon Block, Martin McDonagh, Mark Ravenhill, Ayub Khan Din, Tamantha Hammerschlag, Jess Walters, Ché Walker, Conor McPherson, Simon Stephens, Richard Bean, Roy Williams, Gary Mitchell, Mick Mahoney, Rebecca Gilman, Christopher Shinn, Kia Corthron, David Gieselmann, Marius von Mayenburg, David Eldridge, Leo Butler, Zinnie Harris, Grae Cleugh, Roland Schimmelpfennig, DeObia Oparei, Enda Walsh, Vassily Sigarev, the Presnyakov Brothers, Marcos Barbosa, Lucy Prebble, John Donnelly and Clare Pollard. This expanded programme of new plays has been made possible through the support of A.S.K. Theater Projects and the Skirball Foundation, The Jerwood Charity, the American Friends of the Royal Court Theatre and many in association with the National Theatre Studio.

In recent years there have been record-breaking productions at the box office, with capacity houses for Joe Penhall's Dumb Show, Conor McPherson's Shining City, Roy Williams' Fallout and Terry Johnson's Hitchcock Blonde.

The refurbished theatre in Sloane Square opened in February 2000, with a policy still inspired by the first artistic director George Devine. The Royal Court is an international theatre for new plays and new playwrights, and the work shapes contemporary drama in Britain and overseas.

AWARDS FOR ROYAL COURT

Jez Butterworth won the 1995 George Devine Award, the Writers' Guild New Writer of the Year Award, the Evening Standard Award for Most Promising Playwright and the Olivier Award for Best Comedy for Mojo.

The Royal Court was the overall winner of the 1995 Prudential Award for the Arts for creativity, excellence, innovation and accessibility. The Royal Court Theatre Upstairs won the 1995 Peter Brook Empty Space Award for innovation and excellence in theatre.

Michael Wynne won the 1996 Meyer-Whitworth Award for The Knocky. Martin McDonagh won the 1996 George Devine Award, the 1996 Writers' Guild Best Fringe Play Award, the 1996 Critics' Circle Award and the 1996 Evening Standard Award for Most Promising Playwright for The Beauty Queen of Leenane. Marina Carr won the 19th Susan Smith Blackburn Prize (1996/7) for Portia Coughlan. Conor McPherson won the 1997 George Devine Award, the 1997 Critics' Circle Award and the 1997 Evening Standard Award for Most Promising Playwright for The Weir. Ayub Khan Din won the 1997 Writers' Guild Awards for Best West End Play and Writers' Guild New Writer of the Year and the 1996 John Whiting Award for East is East (co-production with Tamasha).

At the 1998 Tony Awards, Martin McDonagh's The Beauty Queen of Leenane (co-production with Druid Theatre Company) won four awards including Garry Hynes for Best Director and was nominated for a further two. Eugene Ionesco's The Chairs (co-production with Theatre de Complicite) was nominated for six Tony awards. David Hare won the 1998 Time Out Live Award for Outstanding Achievement and six awards in New York including the Drama League, Drama Desk and New York Critics Circle Award for Via Dolorosa. Sarah Kane won the 1998 Arts Foundation Fellowship in Playwriting. Rebecca Prichard won the 1998 Critics' Circle Award for Most Promising Playwright for Yard Gal (co-production with Clean Break).

Conor McPherson won the 1999 Olivier Award for Best New Play for The Weir. The Royal Court won the 1999 ITI Award for Excellence in International Theatre. Sarah Kane's Cleansed was judged Best Foreign Language Play in 1999 by Theater Heute in Germany. Gary Mitchell won the 1999 Pearson Best Play Award for Trust. Rebecca Gilman was joint winner of the 1999 George Devine Award and won the 1999 Evening Standard Award for Most Promising Playwright for The Glory of Living.

In 1999, the Royal Court won the European theatre prize New Theatrical Realities, presented at Taormina Arte in Sicily, for its efforts in recent years in discovering and producing the work of young British dramatists.

Roy Williams and Gary Mitchell were joint winners of the George Devine Award 2000 for Most Promising Playwright for Lift Off and The Force of Change respectively. At the Barclays Theatre Awards 2000 presented by the TMA, Richard Wilson won the Best Director Award for David Gieselmann's Mr Kolpert and Jeremy Herbert won the Best Designer Award for Sarah Kane's 4.48 Psychosis. Gary Mitchell won the Evening Standard's Charles Wintour Award 2000 for Most Promising Playwright for The Force of Change. Stephen Jeffreys' I Just Stopped by to See the Man won an AT&T: On Stage Award 2000.

David Eldridge's Under the Blue Sky won the Time Out Live Award 2001 for Best New Play in the West End. Leo Butler won the George Devine Award 2001 for Most Promising Playwright for Redundant. Roy Williams won the Evening Standard's Charles Wintour Award 2001 for Most Promising Playwright for Clubland. Grae Cleugh won the 2001 Olivier Award for Most Promising Playwright for Fucking Games. Richard Bean was joint winner of the George Devine Award 2002 for Most Promising Playwright for Under the Whaleback. Caryl Churchill won the 2002 Evening Standard Award for Best New Play for A Number. Vassily Sigarev won the 2002 Evening Standard Charles Wintour Award for Most Promising Playwright for Plasticine. Ian MacNeil won the 2002 Evening Standard Award for Best Design for A Number and Plasticine. Peter Gill won the 2002 Critics' Circle Award for Best New Play for The York Realist (English Touring Theatre). Ché Walker won the 2003 George Devine Award for Most Promising Playwright for Flesh Wound. Lucy Prebble won the 2003 Critics' Circle Award and the 2004 George Devine Award for Most Promising Playwright for The Sugar Syndrome.

ROYAL COURT BOOKSHOP

The Royal Court bookshop offers a diverse selection of contemporary plays and publications on the theory and practice of modern drama. The staff specialise in assisting with the selection of audition monologues and scenes.
Royal Court playtexts from past and present productions cost £2.
The Bookshop is situated in the downstairs ROYAL COURT BAR AND FOOD.
Monday–Friday 3–10pm, Saturday 2.30–10pm
For information tel: 020 7565 5024
or email: bookshop@royalcourttheatre.com

PROGRAMME SUPPORTERS

The Royal Court (English Stage Company Ltd) receives its principal funding from Arts Council England, London. It is also supported financially by a wide range of private companies and public bodies and earns the remainder of its income from the box office and its own trading activities. The Royal Borough of Kensington & Chelsea gives an annual grant to the Royal Court Young Writers Programme.

The Genesis Foundation supports the International Season and Young Writers Festival.

The Jerwood Charity supports new plays by new playwrights through the Jerwood New Playwrights series. The Skirball Foundation funds a Playwrights' Programme at the theatre. The Artistic Director's Chair is supported by a lead grant from The Peter Jay Sharp Foundation, contributing to the activities of the Artistic Director's office. Bloomberg Mondays, the Royal Court's reduced price ticket scheme, is supported by Bloomberg. Over the past eight years the BBC has supported the Gerald Chapman Fund for directors.

ROYAL COURT
SLOANE SQUARE

Jerwood Theatre Upstairs
YOUNG PLAYWRIGHTS' SEASON 2004

A Genesis Project

5–20 November 7.45pm
FRESH KILLS
by Elyzabeth Gregory Wilder
Directed by Wilson Milam

26 November–
18 December 7.45pm
A GIRL IN A CAR WITH A MAN
by Rob Evans
Directed by
Joe Hill-Gibbins

Design: Ultz

BOX OFFICE
020 7565 5000
BOOK ONLINE
www.royalcourttheatre.com

FORTY WINKS

Kevin Elyot

For Pauline

But it was even thou, my companion,
my guide, and mine own familiar friend.

Psalm 55: 14

Characters

DON, *thirty-two*

DIANA, *thirty-two*

CHARLIE, *thirty-one*

HOWARD, *thirty-four*

DANNY, *early forties*

HERMIA, *fourteen*

CELIA, *thirteen*

Joni Mitchell's 'A Case of You'. At the end of the first chorus, lights up on:

SCENE ONE

A hotel bedroom, high up, functional and impersonal. Late afternoon, very hot. The music cross-fades with traffic and an intermittent road drill. A double bed and a mini-bar. The bathroom door is closed. A man's jacket, damp with sweat, hangs from the back of a chair in front of a whirring portable fan. DON, in dark trousers, shirt open, has just let in DIANA. She wears a dark suit. They stare at each other like rabbits in headlights.

DON. Did I forget something?

DIANA. No. It's just that I was –

DON. What?

DIANA. Are you alright?

DON. Yes. Are you?

DIANA. Yes. You seem a bit –

DON. I thought you were room service.

DIANA. No.

   Beat.

   I'd better go.

DON. Was there something in particular that – ?

DIANA. No. Do you think I could –

DON. What?

DIANA. – have a drink or something?

DON. There's no ice.

She glances at the mini-bar.

It's broken. They're sending a man up.

DIANA. In this weather . . .

DON. Yes.

DIANA. I shouldn't be here, should I? I don't know what's got into me. It's all too awful, isn't it? A terrible strain, the whole thing.

The thunderous roar of a passing pantechnicon.

Your eulogy was – very moving.

DON. Good. Thank you.

DIANA. 'Everything lapses into oblivion with every extinguished life.' Beautiful. Really lovely. Was that from – ?

DON. No. No, it wasn't.

DIANA. Fancy stipulating in the will that you were to do it! After all this time!

DON *takes out a handkerchief and wipes the sweat from his neck.*

Are you expecting someone?

DON. No.

DIANA. It's just that you –

DON. What?

DIANA. – seem on edge.

An ambulance siren screeches past.

Not very effective, is it? The double-glazing.

DON. Oh. No.

Beat.

I've got a bit of – bit of a stomach thing, actually. Probably one of those canapés at the – do, y'know, what with the – heat and –

DIANA. The anchovy.

DON. Yes, yes, I think it was that. And I'm very tired –
exhausted.

DIANA. Were you trying to sleep?

DON. Well . . .

DIANA. I'm sorry. I shouldn't have come. Sorry.

Beat.

I'd better go.

A thud from the bathroom.

What was that?

DON. What?

DIANA (*re. the bathroom*). Is someone in there?

DON. No, no. It's the plumbing. It sort of – thuds every now
and then. They're – they're sending a man up to do that, too.

DIANA. You should've stayed with us, you know.

DON. Yes, maybe I should have.

DIANA. Or at your mum's.

DON. I didn't want to.

DIANA. No, of course not. But The Brent Cross Leisure
Lodge . . .

Beat.

So you're off – ?

DON. Tomorrow.

DIANA. Tomorrow. Right.

Beat.

I'd better get back – I suppose. Hermia's popped round to a
friend – she's quite upset – and the old-boy contingent's
getting stuck into the spirits and – very loyal, you lot.

They look at each other for a second.

You will be back, won't you?

DON. Yes. Maybe. Sometime.

DIANA. I can't believe I've done this. I am sorry.

DON. Please, don't be.

DIANA. It's just that – I didn't want to be alone.

Beat. She's about to go, then:

Something you said the other Sunday. It could have been such a lovely day, if it hadn't been for the – for the death, but before then it was – rather beautiful, in a way – with you turning up like that and everything.

Beat. She kisses him, first with tenderness, then passion. He responds courteously. Beat.

It was something you said – but I must have misunderstood.

She steps to the door and is about to open it.

Coca-Cola.

DON. What?

DIANA. Good for upset stomachs.

DON. Oh. Yes.

She turns the handle.

DIANA. I'll never forget the back row of the Continental.

She goes, shutting the door behind her. He darts to the bathroom, but just before he gets there, the phone rings. He shoots round in panic. Blackout and distant thunder. Lights up on:

SCENE TWO

*The roofed verandah of a house through which we see a
garden and the Heath beyond. In the garden, under a huge
umbrella, are canvas chairs and a table. The detritus of a
Sunday afternoon, including wine bottles, food and newspapers.
Late afternoon, overcast. DIANA has just entered with DON.
He has a carrier bag. CHARLIE and HOWARD stare at him
from the table. DANNY is dozing. They're drinking wine.*

CHARLIE. Blimey!

DIANA. Can you believe it? It must be –

DON. Fourteen years.

DIANA. Fourteen!

DON. Yes.

DIANA. You look –

HOWARD. Fourteen years older.

DIANA. No, no. You're – just the same. (*Taking his bag off
him.*) Let me.

DON. Oh. Right –

DIANA (*putting it out of the way*). I thought you were Hermia.
That's our daughter. Did you know we had a daughter?

CHARLIE. Blimey!

DIANA. I thought she'd forgotten her key. She should've been
back ages ago.

CHARLIE. Just like her mum.

DON. Really?

DIANA. So they say. She's just turned fourteen.

HOWARD. How did you find us?

DON. The directory. I was in the vicinity, so I thought I'd –
pop by, but – (*Re. CHARLIE.*) – I didn't expect –

HOWARD. He's always turning up, like the proverbial –

DIANA. We're going to the lakeside concert up at Snakewood House, having a picnic with a few friends. Why don't you come?

DON. Oh, no, no, I –

DIANA. You must – (*To* HOWARD.) Mustn't he? (*Back to* DON.) All the old favourites: Rossini, Vivaldi –

CHARLIE. No Joni Mitchell, I'm afraid.

HOWARD. Joni Mitchell!

DIANA (*to* DON). I've still got that tape you made.

DON. Have you?

DIANA. Yes.

HOWARD. Fucking hippy!

DIANA. I'm not absolutely sure where, but –

A brief snore from DANNY.

CHARLIE. That's Danny, my cardiologist. (*Handing him a glass of wine.*) Cheers!

DON. Cheers!

CHARLIE (*toasting*). The iron heart of England!

DON. God!

They drink.

DIANA. Oh, I couldn't wait to get out!

HOWARD. Just as well Dad moved the business down here.

DON. I haven't been back since –

DIANA. You wouldn't recognise it. A one-way system, that's all it is, leading from one mall to the next.

CHARLIE. Fabulous shops, mind you.

DIANA. Everything gone. Even the Continental.

HOWARD. The Continental?

CHARLIE. That fleapit on Hardman Street.

DIANA. The street's gone, too.

DON. Shame.

DIANA. Yes.

Beat, as they sip their drinks.

HOWARD. Your folks still up there?

DON. No. Mum moved down here after Dad died.

DIANA. I'm sorry to hear that.

DON. Yes. She wanted to be near her sister. Unfortunately –

CHARLIE. Now wait a minute, your dad – he travelled a lot, didn't he?

DON. That's right. He sold scent and stuff.

CHARLIE. Yes, I remember! He showed me his samples once: a case full of bottles of . . .

DON. Scent.

CHARLIE. Yes.

HOWARD. Our dad died.

DIANA. Just after their mother, poor woman. It was terrible. No warning. She just dropped dead, mid-sentence. I think that's what killed him.

HOWARD. What are you talking about? It was lung cancer.

DIANA. Caused by grief.

HOWARD. And fifty fags a day.

DIANA. He couldn't speak for grief! He was choked by it!

HOWARD. And a lungful of tar.

DIANA. You never understood.

HOWARD. Course I did.

CHARLIE. They're dead, whatever.

Beat.

DON. Hard to come to terms with, isn't it? In fact, I was –

Thunder, closer. They glance up at the sky.

CHARLIE. Orphans in the storm!

DIANA. They'll have to cancel at this rate.

HOWARD (*under his breath*). With any luck.

DIANA. Why the hell isn't she back? I just can't handle it if she's . . . (*To* DON.) Oh, it's so good to see you!

She pecks his cheek.

CHARLIE. The star-crossed lovers.

DON. For a while.

DIANA (*to* HOWARD *and* CHARLIE). Do you know, the first time we met, he offered me his hand?

CHARLIE. In marriage?

HOWARD. To shake, you prat.

DIANA. I think that's the first time anyone had done that. Well, I'd have only been – what, fourteen, fifteen? I was so – charmed.

DON (*lightly*). Upbringing.

HOWARD. Yeah.

DIANA. Such a gent.

CHARLIE. Remember when I caught you behind the chapel with your tongue down her throat?

DIANA. The fives courts.

CHARLIE. No, it was the chapel. I nearly died.

DON. Sure!

CHARLIE. No, really.

HOWARD. It was *me* who caught you behind the fives courts.

DON. And put me in detention.

HOWARD. Did I?

DON. Yes.

CHARLIE. Probably jealous.

DIANA. And we used to skive off for coffee –

CHARLIE. – and I'd follow you.

DON. Did you?

CHARLIE. Sometimes.

DIANA. – and then sneak into the Continental and sit in the back row and get up to all sorts.

CHARLIE. I never knew that.

DIANA. Oh, yes. That's where we had our first serious snog –

CHARLIE. What do you mean, serious?

DIANA. I mean, serious, and once, during some Italian movie . . .

Beat.

CHARLIE. What?

DIANA. Oh, it was just – something . . .

CHARLIE. What?

DIANA. . . . . in the film. Of course, I didn't see most of it, but there was some nice Mozart and a dishy guy in tight trousers –

DON. Terence Stamp.

DIANA. – and a maid who levitated.

DON. *Theorem.*

DIANA. That's the one.

HOWARD. Sounds a barrel of laughs.

DIANA. And you were supposed to be writing an essay.

HOWARD. Was that when you nicked the book?

DON. Yes.

DIANA. And you cribbed from it to get your essay in on time,
then someone ratted on you –

DON. That's right.

DIANA. – and you were –

DON. – beaten –

DIANA. Yes.

DON. – and threatened with expulsion because the Head was
told I was part of a gang of shoplifters, which I wasn't, but
no one believed me, and no one stood up for me, and he
informed my parents, and they were so ashamed that they
couldn't bring themselves to show their faces at Speech
Day, where I was due to receive a prize. They'd have been
so proud. It was what they'd worked for all their lives, to
see me succeed where they hadn't been able to, and because
of a lie, their hearts were broken.

Beat.

HOWARD. But you did nick a book.

DON. Out of panic, and only the once, to get the essay done,
but it was the 'regular thief' tag that stuck, that did the
damage at school and at home – as I'm sure you all
remember.

A muffled rumble of thunder.

HOWARD. You win some, you lose some.

A moment's hiatus, then:

DIANA. Just need to finish the hamper. I'll only be a minute.
(*Pointing to DON's empty glass.*) Howard . . .

CHARLIE. I'll give you a hand.

*They've gone, leaving DON and HOWARD uncomfortably
together. HOWARD tops him up. DANNY's still dozing.*

HOWARD. So what've you been up to?

DON. This and that.

HOWARD. Expansive as ever.

DON. Cheers.

HOWARD. Yeah.

They drink.

DON. You?

HOWARD. Cape and Sons. Naturally. Can't seem to escape the old man's clutches even with him scattered to the four winds.

DON. You don't like it?

HOWARD. It's the board meetings that piss me off, surrounded by the same old tossers I passed the orange with at Christmas parties. Like a recurring nightmare. Charlie jumped ship, of course, a couple of years after Dad kicked the bucket.

DON. What does he do now?

HOWARD. He claims to be writing a play, but seems to spend most of his time getting laid. I think he sees it as the last days of Sodom.

A snore from DANNY.

(*Re.* DANNY.) Would you put your life in his hands?

They smile and take a sip.

(*Re. the wine.*) What d'you reckon?

DON (*swilling it round the glass and sniffing*). . . . Summery, I'd say.

HOWARD. Summery?

DON. Yes.

HOWARD. Would that be – croquet-on-the-lawn summery, or frazzled-on-a-beach?

DON (*another sniff*). . . . Hazy . . . Kind of English . . .

HOWARD. More sort of . . . crack-of-ball-on-wood?

DON. Yes.

HOWARD. Yes. (*Sniffing.*) I'd say . . . scarcely memorable.

DON. What is it?

HOWARD. The *vin du jour*, according to Diana. She's ordered cratefuls of the stuff from Bibendum. We'll be drinking it for years. (*Sniffing.*) Don't you detect just the . . . slightest nuance of asparagus piss?

DON. Y'know, since you mention it –

HOWARD. I'm right, aren't I?

DON. Yes.

HOWARD. Yes . . .

> *They share a chuckle, which fades swiftly into the dusky air. Silence.*

It's Lebanese.

> *Beat.*

Didn't you want to be a vicar?

DON. I read Theology but, no, I don't think I ever saw myself as a vicar.

HOWARD. Theology –

DON. – and Electrical Engineering. I dropped out –

HOWARD. Not surprised.

DON. – and flirted with the Merchant Navy before landing a job with the WHO. I went all over – Kenya, Malawi, Ethiopia – but eventually it wore me down, so I packed it in and taught History for a year in Tasmania –

HOWARD. Tasmania?

DON. The Princess Elizabeth College for Girls – then bummed around for a while, with the occasional trip to London, before fetching up in Rome where, for the moment, I teach Cultural Studies to rich Americans.

HOWARD. I've sometimes wondered what that must be like –

DON. An uphill struggle, believe me.

HOWARD. – following your nose through life. No ties. Free to go wherever. More glamorous than flogging cricket gear, I'm damned sure of that.

DON. One place is very like another after a while. It's still the same hangover. The same itch in the groin.

HOWARD. The Princess Elizabeth College for Girls, eh?

DON. I've never really settled, never really felt, 'Ah yes, this is it. I've arrived. Home at last.'

HOWARD. Fourteen years! Jesus! Like I've been treading water all this time.

DON. Diana okay?

HOWARD. Unstoppable. She's with Apex now.

DON. Is that – ?

HOWARD. Trendy chambers with a penchant for defending Irish terrorists and other reprobates. Earns a bomb.

DON. How is she – in herself?

HOWARD. You'll have to ask her. And *we*, which is probably what you're getting round to, we couldn't be happier.

DON. Good.

HOWARD. As happy as we'll ever be.

DON. Right.

HOWARD. God, I hate summer!

Beat.

Every morning I wake up and hear her clipping away at something with her fucking secateurs. When I think how it used to be . . . Oh, Donald, the littleness of life! Found anyone yet?

DON *shrugs.*

We still don't like each other, do we?

CHARLIE *enters.*

CHARLIE (*to* HOWARD). Diana wants a word.

HOWARD leaves.

Big brother! Ever the dickhead, but what can you do?

DANNY grunts.

DON. Aren't you well?

CHARLIE. How do you mean?

DON (*re.* DANNY). You said he was your cardiologist.

CHARLIE. Ah, that. Yes, heart disease. It was the family firm that did for me. Best decision I ever made, walking out of that place. Imagine, me working in cricket gear. The only highlight was when I prototyped a specially ventilated box. They're still selling, I believe.

DON. And your heart?

CHARLIE. Alright. Bit of angina, nothing much. (*Re.* DANNY.) He did my angioplasty. Heroic! The way he slid that catheter up my artery, I thought I'd gone to heaven, and since then . . .

DON. So you and . . . ?

CHARLIE. Danny. Yes, we are.

DON. Have you been together long?

CHARLIE. Yes. Coming up to two months. He's a bit wary, of course – Belfast – but quite a goer when he puts his mind to it. Ejaculates like a birthing sea-horse. And *your* heart?

DON. What about it?

CHARLIE. Still there, is it? Not stolen, or broken?

DON. No.

Beat.

CHARLIE. I'm trying my hand at writing, you know. A play.

DON. Yes, Howard said.

CHARLIE. He's not very happy about it. Thinks I've betrayed him, but it's what I've always wanted to do, and with things

as they are . . . Well, you've got to give it a go, haven't you?
Might not get another opportunity. And it gives me the
chance to sort of – squirt my spray on the lamp post of
immortality.

DON. What's it about?

CHARLIE. Hard to say. It's quite – ambitious, though. I'm
trying for something a bit – mysterious . . .

DON. A thriller?

CHARLIE. No. Mysterious in a – spiritual way. Kind of –
transcendent – sort of thing.

DON. Right. How's it going?

CHARLIE. Bit slow. In fact I'm still on the opening speech.
There's a word I've been struggling with for weeks.

DON. What is it?

CHARLIE. Well, if I knew . . .

DON. Of course.

CHARLIE. It's that moment when something's about to – how
can I put it? – about to come to fruition.

DON. Budding?

CHARLIE. No. No, that's not quite right. It's more –

DON. Tumescent?

CHARLIE. Ooh, well. I see where you're coming from, but it's
more sort of –

DON. Fruitive.

CHARLIE. Ye-es, but –

DON. If it's 'coming to fruition' you want.

CHARLIE. Well, it is. It is what I want: 'fruitive'. Yes, in a
way . . . Yes . . . Difficult, isn't it? But I'm determined to
get it right. It's worth it, don't you think? You've got to give
things your best shot.

DANNY *snores*.

DON. He likes his sleep.

CHARLIE. We had a bit of a night of it. Went to this new club in Spitalfields called The Cheese Counter. I think it used to be an old dairy. Well, I say club, more of a – hole, really. Lots of strange noises and worrying smells. Hands all over you. Someone stuck his tongue down my throat at one point. Dreadful case of oral warts. It was like licking pebbledash. (*Re.* DANNY.) And this one overdid the ketamine – not for the first time, may I say. (*Sotto voce.*) Friends in the pharmacy.

DIANA pops in.

DIANA. I'm so sorry about this, Don, we're running terribly late. We'll miss the concert at this rate, and if Hermia doesn't turn up soon . . .

She's gone.

CHARLIE. Hasn't aged too well, has she? And she and Howard . . . Separate rooms, you know.

Distant thunder. They glance up at the sky.

Doesn't look too promising. Now, Hermia: she's the spit of Diana – as she was.

DON. Is she?

CHARLIE. Oh, yes. She might turn out alright, if Di doesn't stifle her to death. Far too protective.

DON. Isn't that natural?

CHARLIE. Sort of, but you see, about a year ago, something happened.

DON. Oh?

CHARLIE. Yes. Hermia was up on the Heath and – well, they thought she may have been molested, but she can't remember, and the general consensus is that she probably dropped off and had some sort of dream. But ever since –

DANNY shifts his position, revealing a prominent erection straining beneath his trousers. They both clock it.

Oh dear. It's been like that since we got up. He mistook some strange new stimulant for an antacid. I've blown him off twice, but . . .

They continue to look at it.

Doctors!

HOWARD (*off*). Charlie!

CHARLIE. What?

HOWARD (*off*). Clear the table, will you?

CHARLIE. Thinks he's still a prefect.

> CHARLIE *starts clearing the table.* DON *vaguely assists.*

DON. Always looked out for his little brother, though, didn't he?

CHARLIE. Sometimes a little too much.

DON. How do you mean?

CHARLIE. Well, he wasn't averse to a bit of how's-your-father.

DON. Really?

CHARLIE. Taught me a trick or two, I tell you.

Some moments of silent clearing up.

You looked out for me too, didn't you?

DON. Did I?

CHARLIE. Even though I was the year below. You didn't look down on me. You were kind. You don't forget that.

Beat.

So are you around for a while?

DON. No. I'm off back to Rome tomorrow.

CHARLIE. Rome?

DON. I teach there.

CHARLIE. Nice.

DON. Yes.

More moments of silent clearing.

CHARLIE. I was wondering . . .

DON. What?

CHARLIE. Perhaps we might catch a moment together before
. . . before you –

DON. Well, it's –

HOWARD (*off*). Charlie!

CHARLIE (*shouting*). I'm doing it!

They continue the clearing up.

Y'know, when I caught you and Diana snogging at school
all those years ago, I nearly died.

DON. Yes, you said.

CHARLIE. No, but really. I started hyperventilating. I thought
I'd pass out.

DON. I didn't know.

CHARLIE. Why should you? But I think you knew I carried a
torch for you, didn't you?

DON. I'm not so special.

CHARLIE. You are, though. Everyone thought so. Perhaps
because you keep yourself hidden. I was besotted, but I
knew I was onto a losing wicket. Well, you weren't gay, for
one thing.

DON. No.

CHARLIE. You weren't, were you?

DON. No, I wasn't.

CHARLIE. And still aren't, I suppose.

DON. That's right.

CHARLIE. Right. Meeting you again, it's like it's never gone
away.

He glances at DANNY.

It'd be a shame – not to see each other again.

DON. With me on the move all the time –

CHARLIE. We were best mates.

DON. But you've got your own life now. You've got Danny.

CHARLIE. Danny. Yes, well . . . (*Lowering his voice.*) I never thought I'd end up like this, y'know, clutching at straws.

DON. You haven't ended up anywhere yet.

CHARLIE. I'm not so sure. The pattern's set, I can tell.

He glances at DANNY *again, then looks back at* DON.

(*Quietly.*) You've still got the same eyes.

DON. Well, I suppose I would have, wouldn't I?

CHARLIE. The same mouth.

Another glance at DANNY.

(*Almost a whisper.*) Kiss me. Kiss me like you kissed her.

They look at each other for a moment.

HOWARD (*off*). Charlie!

Beat. CHARLIE *walks out with a tray full of things.* DON *breathes a sigh of relief and looks out at the garden.*

DANNY (*Belfast. Without opening his eyes*). So then, you were a regular shirtlifter.

DON *spins round.* DANNY *opens his eyes.*

DON. What?

DANNY. At school.

DON. I think you mean shoplifter.

DANNY. Is that right?

DON. No, it isn't.

DANNY. There was a lot of it at my school – shoplifting. And shirtlifting too, for that matter.

DON. I was not a shoplifter. I took a book – once – out of desperation.

DANNY. Books, eh? I was a booze-and-fags man myself – and the occasional piece of electrical equipment. Wrote the odd dodgy essay, too – only difference, I got away with it. What's on your mind?

DON. Nothing.

Beat.

DANNY. So then, you're a friend of the family?

DON. No. I popped in on the off-chance.

DANNY. After fourteen years?

DON. You heard that bit as well.

DANNY *hits his erection.*

DANNY. Families! If there's one thing worse than your own, it's other people's. All those secret signs and codes – like the fucking Masons. And relationships! The surreptitious squeeze, the knowing whisper. I tell you, I'm happiest in the theatre –

DON. I never find the time.

DANNY. – performing my little procedures, when the buggers are on their own and they've only me to rely on.

DON. You're not that fond of people, then?

DANNY. I've never found much need for them. When I was a kid, it was my pets kept me company, but the bastards kept dying on me. Ended up with a couple of stick insects – Funk and Wagnall. Now those two, faithful to the last. Hardly the life and soul, mind you; just nibbled bits of privet.

DON. What about Charlie?

DANNY. Nice lad.

DON. Yes. One of the good guys.

DANNY. Suppose so.

DON. Decent. A man of his word.

DANNY. When he can find it.

DON. Don't you find much need for him?

DANNY. Probably not.

Beat.

DON. I wonder if . . .

DANNY. What?

DON. Well, the thing is, I've not been – not been sleeping too
well lately – for years, to tell you the truth – and I was
wondering if you – if you might be able to – suggest
something, seeing as you . . . I've tried moving my bed, and
putting a plank under the mattress. Sleeping pills, of course,
but I got addicted and had to see a counsellor. I've tried
exercise, getting up, not going to bed, warm baths. I've
avoided alcohol, siestas, TV, too much work. I've tried
imagination games – actually, that did work once or twice.

DANNY. What did you imagine?

DON. It was more a case of . . .

Beat.

. . . more a case of – remembering, I suppose, but I began
to find the memories – well . . . So do you?

DANNY. What?

DON. Have anything – to suggest?

DANNY. Not my field.

DON *turns away. Beat.*

So then, you're up on the Heath, and it suddenly comes into
your head to pop in on some people, who aren't particular
friends of yours, that you haven't seen for fourteen years
and you don't even know where they live.

DON. That's about the size of it.

DANNY. And you have to look them up in the directory.

DON. You weren't asleep at all, were you?

DANNY (*hitting his erection again*). Fucking thing!

DON. I've been having – having quite a time of it lately.

DANNY. Right.

DON. Needed some space to think, that's all. Death throws you back on yourself. You should know that in your line of work.

DANNY. Someone's died, have they?

DON. Yes.

DANNY. Who?

DON. My mother.

DANNY. Right.

Distant thunder. They look up at the sky.

Michael Fish. What a cunt!

DON. And then Diana, when I was up on the Heath – she came to mind. We were at school together – well, she was at the girls' school, I was at the – boys'. Up in the Midlands.

DANNY. Right.

DON. She used to mean a lot to me, you see – everything – and I thought, seeing her again might be a comfort.

DANNY. Now there's a girl! (*Adjusting his erection.*) You wouldn't flick it with a pencil, would you? Never works when I do it myself.

DON. I'd rather not.

DANNY. You're sure now?

DON. Not my field.

They look at each other.

DANNY. And is it what you thought it might be, seeing her again?

Beat.

DON. Diana – she was life and death to me. Then Howard stepped in. He was a couple of years older, a prefect, and took against me from the first.

DANNY. That guy, he deserves himself.

DON. It was him who shopped me – never admitted it, of course – and then he went about stealing her from me. (*Touching his head.*) She's here, all the time, just as she was.

DANNY. Why come back? Why not leave it alone?

DON. I wanted – wanted to – to see her.

He looks out at the garden. DANNY *watches him.*

DANNY. You won't get away with it, y'know.

DON *turns to him as* DIANA *enters.*

DIANA (*to* DANNY). Oh, good, you're up.

DANNY. Better go to the bathroom, sort myself out.

He goes out.

DIANA. All I need now is my daughter. Why does she do this to me? I'm so sorry to leave you like that.

DON. It's okay.

DIANA (*looking at him*). It's the strangest thing – like it was yesterday.

She touches his cheek.

Are you alright? What is it? Don, what's wrong?

DON. I'm tired . . . Tired, that's all.

DIANA. Have a sleep.

DON. That's the problem: I can't. I haven't slept properly in years.

DIANA. Well, try. Rest. Stay here. There's no need to come with us. Stay here and rest. Stay the night. You'd be so welcome.

DON. I need to stop –

DIANA. Yes.

DON. – but I don't know where.

DIANA. Here. You can stop here.

DON. There's no one left, you see. Just you. How we were.

DIANA. I think about it, too.

DON. Why did you do it? Why did you go off with him?

DIANA. It's – the way it happened.

DON. Yes –

DIANA. I hope it brightens up.

DON. – and now we've all moved on – in our own ways. You don't even love each other, do you?

DIANA. We did.

DON. For how long, though? How long did you love each other?

DIANA. I don't know. We were – young, we were –

DON. I'd still love you.

DIANA. You don't know that.

DON. Oh yes, I do. I'm quite sure I would. Why did you do it?

DIANA. There are days, I swear to you, when I wish I hadn't.

He stares at her.

DON. Diana . . .

DIANA. Yes?

DON. Dido . . .

DIANA (*remembering*). Dido . . .

DON (*almost whispered*). Di . . .

A rustling of leaves as a breeze disturbs the trees, then silence.

Mum's dead, you know.

DIANA. Oh, Don, I'm so sorry.

DON. Two weeks ago.

DIANA. Poor darling!

DON. Yes. Well . . .

DIANA. If ever you want to talk . . .

He nods, suddenly unable to speak.

(*Embracing him.*) Don . . .

She holds him, then breaks the embrace. She looks out at the garden.

I love this place in summer. It keeps things in perspective. (*Glancing at the sky.*) Do you know, I think it might be . . . (*Looking at him.*) Don't ever feel alone. (*Embracing him again.*) It's now that matters, isn't it? Now. This moment.

She looks into his eyes and strokes his hair.

And even this is already a memory.

She gently kisses his lips.

What stupid creatures we are!

DON *remains passive in her embrace. Enter* HOWARD, CHARLIE *and* DANNY, *his erection gone. They each clock* DON *and* DIANA. HOWARD *starts trying, unsuccessfully, to take down the umbrella,* CHARLIE *loads a tray with what's left on the table, and* DANNY *has a cigarette.*

CHARLIE. . . . . It's that moment when something's about to –

HOWARD. – come to fruition. Yes, you've told me!

CHARLIE. Keep your hair on!

HOWARD. I don't see why you're that bothered, anyway. Actors say what they want, don't they?

CHARLIE. My scripts aren't suggestions, you know. I don't write the gist.

HOWARD. So what's it about?

CHARLIE. Look, I know you're trying to show an interest –

HOWARD. I want to know.

CHARLIE. – but you don't have to, really.

HOWARD. Tell me.

CHARLIE. Well – it's hard to say.

HOWARD. Why?

CHARLIE. Because it's about –

HOWARD. What?

CHARLIE. – quite a big issue, I suppose.

HOWARD. What d'you mean, big? What's big?

CHARLIE. Like – you know –

HOWARD. No, I don't fucking know. That's why I'm asking.

CHARLIE. – mysterious.

HOWARD. A thriller?

CHARLIE. No, not a thriller! More a – spiritual kind of
approach to –

HOWARD. What?!

CHARLIE. Love.

He quickly glances at DON.

HOWARD. Eh?

CHARLIE. That's what it's about.

HOWARD. Love?

CHARLIE. Sort of.

HOWARD. What, you mean, like – sex?

CHARLIE. No. Love.

Beat.

HOWARD. Well, that'll have them queueing round the block.

CHARLIE. You see!

HOWARD. 'Ooh, a play about love!'

CHARLIE. You just don't understand, do you?

HOWARD. 'So what'll we do tonight? Go down the pub and stare at the barmaid's tits, or sit in the dark for two hours and watch a play about love?'

CHARLIE. No poetry, that's your problem, mate.

HOWARD (*suddenly turning*). Mate? Don't call me mate! Is this what you've left the firm for? A mysterious kind of spiritual sort of play about love that doesn't have any fucking sex in it? Don't mate me! You've dumped me right in it! Right – mate?

CHARLIE (*quietly*). Right.

Beat. CHARLIE *returns to his clearing up,* HOWARD *to his struggle with the umbrella.*

DANNY. Plant.

CHARLIE. What?

DANNY. That's your word: plant.

CHARLIE. What do you mean, 'plant'?

DANNY. Plants bud, come to fruition. That's your word: plant.

CHARLIE. You can't say something's 'plant'.

DANNY. But you can say something's 'a plant'.

CHARLIE. I am describing a young lad, Danny. I have told you this. I cannot write, 'Melvyn was a plant.'

DANNY. Theatre! What's the fucking point?

CHARLIE. The point is, it can give you what you can't actually have – that's the point!

He takes a full tray into the house, clocking DON *and* DIANA *still embracing. Distant thunder.*

HOWARD. Hear that, Diana?

DIANA (*extricating herself from the embrace*). You'll have to dig out the groundsheet.

HOWARD (*under his breath*). Bloody picnic!

DIANA. And the kagools. They're in the cloakroom somewhere.

HOWARD (*still under his breath*). Bloody concert!

DIANA. Who knows? You might enjoy it.

The umbrella suddenly collapses on him.

For God's sake, Howard! The concert starts in ten minutes!

DANNY (*helping him out from under it*). Y'alright, now?

DIANA. Have you sorted the wine yet?

HOWARD (*to DANNY, emerging from under the umbrella*). Thanks, mate.

DIANA. The Lebanese white – what do you think?

HOWARD *stomps off*, DANNY *following*. DON *and* DIANA *are left alone, suddenly self-conscious. A thin shaft of sunlight has broken through, casting a shadow across the garden.*

He always has to make such a song and dance about it.

Beat.

Are you going to be alright? (*Before he can answer.*) At last!

She's spotted HERMIA *approaching the house through the garden.* HERMIA's *wearing a short cotton dress.* DIANA *rushes to meet her. As she brings her up onto the verandah:*

Where have you been?

HERMIA. With Daphne.

DIANA. I've been worried sick.

HERMIA. She's got this new kite.

DIANA. Why didn't you call?

HERMIA. It's so cool.

DIANA. We're going to be late because of you.

HERMIA. It goes like a rocket and we crashed it into someone's picnic –

DIANA. Where?

HERMIA. – and they were like seriously cross and we were pissing ourselves.

DIANA. Where was this?

HERMIA. Mum, I really don't want to go to this concert.

DIANA. Where were you?

HERMIA. I want to stay here.

DIANA. Tell me where you were!

HERMIA. Can I?

DIANA. What?

HERMIA. Stay here. There's something I want to see on the telly. Oh please, Mum!

DIANA. I want to know where you were.

HERMIA. And those concerts are so boring. I hate them.

DIANA. You're not staying or going anywhere till you tell me.

HERMIA. Up on the hill.

DIANA. The hill?

HERMIA. We had the best time.

DIANA. On the Heath?

HERMIA. Yes. I *told* you that's where I was going.

DIANA. You didn't.

HERMIA. I did.

DIANA. Hermia, you didn't tell me. I've told you *never* to go up there.

HERMIA. I was with Daphne.

DIANA. Never! You promised.

HERMIA. I didn't.

DIANA. You did!

   HERMIA *clocks* DON.

   This is Don, an old friend from school.

DON. Hi.

   He offers his hand. She looks at it. A nervous giggle, then:

HERMIA. Oh, Mum, I want a kite like Daphne's. You should
   see it. It's just –

   Her head falls forward. DIANA *reaches out and holds her.*

DIANA. Darling, you're –

HERMIA. – wicked. All –

   Her head lolls back. Her legs give way.

DIANA. Oh, my darling –

DON. What is it?

HERMIA (*momentarily coming to*). – silvery . . .

   She passes out. DIANA *helps her to a chair. Beat.*

DON. What's wrong?

DIANA. It's come on in the past year. A sort of – narcolepsy.
   At first they thought it might be MS, but it isn't, thank God.

DON. What brought it on?

DIANA. Nothing very much, or so it seems. She'd been up on
   the Heath, and I thought someone had attacked her, but tests
   were done, questions asked, and all they could surmise was
   that she'd fallen asleep and had a dream. She does say –
   odd things from time to time, but . . . Hormonal stirrings,
   that's probably it.

DON. Is there anything you can do?

DIANA. No one seems to know much about it. I recently
dragged her and Howard along to a narcoleptics' self-help
group.

DON. What happened?

DIANA. Not a lot. Quite relaxing, though.

HERMIA (*coming to*). . . . He came to me . . . like an angel . . .

DIANA (*stroking her hair*). You dreamt it, darling. It was a
dream.

HERMIA. . . . touched me, and said . . .

She drops off again.

DON. How long will she be like this?

DIANA. They don't know. We'll just have to . . .

Beat.

DON. If you want, I could – stay here, if she – Hermia doesn't
want to go. I'm not really in the mood for music. I could
stay – till you got back. If you wanted.

DIANA. That would be –

DON. I'd quite like to. It's peaceful here, isn't it? It'd be nice
to – stare at the garden for an hour or two. It's been quite
a day. I'd intended scattering my mother's ashes, but when
it came to it . . .

DIANA. You poor thing.

DON. She'd only been up on the Heath a couple of times – not
that handy for her, really – but she decided that's where she
wanted them scattered.

They look at each other.

I'll do it another day, I suppose.

HOWARD (*off*). Diana!

DIANA. I know we were young, but – it was very special,
wasn't it – what we had?

DON. Yes. It was – as you say.

DIANA. If we could only step back . . .

DON. Yes.

HOWARD (*off*). Come on!

DON. So shall I?

DIANA. What?

DON. Stay? Just until you get back?

DIANA. Thank you. (*Re.* HERMIA.) You don't have to do anything, by the way. She'll just wake up and – she'll be fine.

HOWARD (*off*). For fuck's sake!

DIANA. I ought to go. Help yourself to – whatever.

DON. Yes. I will.

    CHARLIE *enters*.

CHARLIE. Spit-spot!

DIANA. Don's not coming.

CHARLIE. Why not?

DIANA. He's going to keep an eye on Hermia.

CHARLIE. Oh.

    Enter DANNY.

DANNY. He said he'll give us twenty seconds.

DIANA (*to* DON). See you later.

    She pecks his cheek and leaves.

DANNY. Got out of it, have you?

CHARLIE. He's staying with Hermia.

DANNY. Right.

    He gives DON *a look and leaves.*

CHARLIE. See you, then.

DON. Yes.

CHARLIE *gives him a hesitant smile and makes to go,*
then:

CHARLIE. 'If I might choose, I'd rather die – '

DON. ' – Than be one day debarred thy company.'

CHARLIE. You remember!

DON. 'He only lives that deadly is in love.' Drayton. Poet
Laureate.

CHARLIE. The night before he died.

The impatient hooting of a car horn. CHARLIE *leaves.*
DON *doesn't move. Quiet.* HERMIA's *still sleeping. He*
looks out at the garden and breathes deeply, then he picks
up a discarded newspaper. He flops into a chair on the
opposite side of the verandah from HERMIA *and starts*
to browse through it. He glances out at the garden again,
then returns to the paper. He turns a page. Pause. He turns
another page. Pause. Then another. Beat. For the first time
he peers over the top of the paper at the sleeping HERMIA.
He gazes at her for a few seconds, then returns his attention
to the paper. He turns another page. Pause. In the distance,
drifting across from the Heath, we hear the opening of
Rossini's 'The Thieving Magpie' overture. He looks in the
direction of the music, listens, then returns to the paper. The
music continues as he reads. Then, once again, he peers
over the top at HERMIA. *Beat. He returns to the paper. He*
turns a page. Beat. Again, he peers over the top of the
paper at HERMIA. *Pause. He slowly puts the paper down,*
all the time watching her, and carries on watching her as
the lights gradually fade. The Rossini continues until the
lights come up on:

SCENE THREE

The hotel room the second after the end of Scene One. DON at the bathroom door, staring at the ringing phone. Outside, the sounds of speeding traffic and intermittent drilling. The portable fan whirrs away. He doesn't move a muscle. The phone eventually stops. He opens the bathroom door and disappears inside. Beat. He comes out, HERMIA's body draped across his arms. He carefully lays her on the bed and strokes her forehead.

DON. Hermia . . . Hermia, wake up . . . Please . . .

He inspects the side of her forehead. He dashes back into the bathroom and returns with a damp flannel. He gently dabs her forehead.

Hermia . . . Hermia . . .

She stirs.

Are you alright?

HERMIA (*groggily*). Mum – where is she?

DON. Gone. She went.

HERMIA. What she want?

DON. Nothing, really. Just – came to say goodbye.

Her head lolls to one side.

Hermia, please . . . Please don't drop off . . . Stay awake . . . Please . . .

She tries to rouse herself, a smile on her face.

That's it, that's a good girl.

HERMIA. I heard her voice, then –

DON. Bang!

HERMIA. Yes.

DON. You've hit your head.

HERMIA. 'T's alright. I'm used to it.

DON. You shouldn't be here.

HERMIA. I wanted to see you.

DON. Your mum'll wonder where you are.

HERMIA. She always wonders where I am.

DON. Why did you come?

HERMIA (*her head lolling against him*). Mm, that's nice . . .

DON. Hermia, tell me.

HERMIA. What?

DON. Why you're here.

HERMIA. Uncle Charlie.

DON. What about him?

HERMIA. Want to know what happened.

DON. He had a heart attack. You know that.

HERMIA. Why?

DON. He had a weak heart.

HERMIA. He wasn't that old.

DON. He wasn't old at all.

HERMIA. It's sad.

DON. Yes. Yes, it is.

HERMIA. I'll always remember Charlie.

DON. So will I.

HERMIA. He shouldn't have died.

DON. No. But it happens.

HERMIA. Why does it happen?

DON. There might not be a reason.

HERMIA. But if there was, what might it be?

DON. I don't know. Too much worry, stress . . .

HERMIA. Surprise?

DON. Could be.

HERMIA. I like surprises.

DON. Yes, but when you've got a weak heart, surprises aren't good for you.

HERMIA. Is your heart weak?

DON. Not in that way. Look, your parents'll be worried sick.

HERMIA. Mum's always worried –

DON. You're fourteen, for God's sake!

HERMIA. – and Dad'll be too pissed.

DON. You've got to go, you really have.

HERMIA. So what was the surprise?

DON. What surprise?

HERMIA. The one that killed Uncle Charlie.

DON. I don't know that he had a surprise.

HERMIA. But if he *did* have one, what might it have been?

DON. I don't know.

HERMIA. They had to turn back on the way to the concert, didn't they?

DON. Yes.

HERMIA. Cos he'd forgotten something.

DON. If you know what happened, why are you asking?

HERMIA. He needed a spray for his vagina –

DON. Angina. He'd forgotten his angina spray.

HERMIA. – and he came in and saw something that surprised him, didn't he?

DON. You tell me.

HERMIA. What was it? What did he see?

DON. Don't play games, Hermia.

A passing, nerve-jangling police siren.

HERMIA. Was he a good friend of yours?

DON. Yes – a while ago.

HERMIA. He must have liked you, cos he wanted you to talk about him at his funeral. Did you like him?

DON. We used to be friends, I've told you.

HERMIA. Will you miss him?

DON. Of course I'll miss him. Now get up. You've got to go. You shouldn't be here.

HERMIA. Just five more minutes, then . . .

Her head lolls forward for a moment.

DON. Hermia . . .

She rallies.

Would you like something to drink, or eat?

HERMIA. It shouldn't have happened. He shouldn't have died.

DON. Please, Hermia!

HERMIA. We made it happen, didn't we?

DON. No. No, of course we didn't.

HERMIA. It's all our fault, all our . . .

Her head lolls forward for a moment.

DON. Hermia . . .

He shakes her. She comes to.

It's not our fault. D'you hear me? It's not our fault. You must believe me.

HERMIA. But if we –

DON. You do believe me, don't you? His heart was weak. He was very sick. At any moment it could've happened. It was how he was, and nothing could change that. It's no one's fault. It's terrible – terrible – but that's the way it is. You do understand that, don't you? You do trust me? Yes?

She nods.

Yes?

She nods again.

Good girl, good girl . . .

She momentarily drops off.

Hermia . . .

HERMIA (*coming to*). . . . Like the time before . . . Came like an angel . . . So beautiful . . . like I could sleep forever . . .

She goes again.

DON (*gently shaking her*). Hermia . . . Hermia . . .

She opens her eyes and looks up into his.

HERMIA. Where have you been?

DON. What?

HERMIA. This past year. Why haven't you been back?

DON. Been back where?

HERMIA. To see me.

DON. I've never seen you before.

HERMIA. Haven't you?

DON. Well, the other Sunday –

HERMIA. No, before that.

Her head lolls forward for a second, then:

I've seen you lots . . .

Her head lolls back, a smile on her face.

DON. Hermia . . . Please . . . What d'you mean, you've seen me lots? . . . Hermia . . .

She's out. The phone rings. He jumps. He stares at it. It keeps ringing. It stops. He looks back at HERMIA, *then darts over to the fridge, takes out a bottle of water and goes back to* HERMIA, *in his haste forgetting to shut the fridge door.*

Hermia . . .

He awkwardly raises her. She starts to come to. He tries to give her some water, but she turns her head away.

Tell me. Tell me what you mean.

HERMIA. . . . . ever since I saw you on the Heath.

DON. When did you see me?

HERMIA. Last year. It was you.

DON. No.

HERMIA. I know it was.

DON. No, it wasn't. It wasn't me.

HERMIA. You came to me, and touched me, and whispered in my ear –

DON. No, Hermia, I didn't. It must have been someone else. You mustn't say these things.

HERMIA. – and the other Sunday –

DON. What about the other Sunday?

HERMIA. – you came to me again –

DON. No.

HERMIA. – and what you did to me, that's how I knew: it was you on the Heath.

DON. It wasn't, I promise.

HERMIA. It was, and ever since, I've dreamt about you.

DON. No. No, you're wrong. It wasn't me.

HERMIA. But it doesn't matter, don't you see?

DON. It does matter. It matters very much.

HERMIA. What you did, what you said –

DON. I did nothing, said nothing.

HERMIA. – I understand.

DON. I never saw you up there, never touched you or whispered in your ear.

HERMIA. I know what it is.

DON. It was someone else –

HERMIA. It's love. It's love, isn't it?

DON. – someone else . . .

HERMIA. No, it wasn't. I know it was you. See, sometimes I might *seem* asleep . . .

She crumples against him, her eyes closed. He tries to rouse her –

DON. Hermia . . . Hermia . . .

– but she's out. He stares at her, then darts over to the window in a panic. He takes out his handkerchief and wipes the sweat from his neck and face. He tries to control his breathing. He looks back at her, still at the window.

It's because of my mother that I was there, that I was on the Heath the other Sunday, and the time before that was because of her, too. I'd come over to see her, as I did every now and then. That's all.

Beat.

That's all.

A sudden burst of drilling.

Everything's fine, normal as ever, then she gets a bit of a cold, then a chest infection, and before you know it, it's pneumonia and she's dead. No time to say what you meant, do what you'd planned . . . I stood looking at her, waiting for a smile, a nod of approval, like I was still a boy, and I thought, 'Is that it? All those years. All that struggle. Is that it?'

HERMIA *sleeps on.*

It was because of her that I was there, because of her.

Another burst of drilling. In a flash he's shut the curtains, the suddenly darkened room lit only by the light from the open fridge door. He stays there, facing the curtains, his back to the bed, as he continues speaking.

But then I saw you – asleep, on the Heath, all alone . . . For years I'd tried to get away, and out of the blue, there you were. You'd come back to me . . .

Another burst of drilling.

And again I tried, for a whole year I tried, but again you were there, playing with your friend, even more like the girl I knew.

He slowly turns.

You won't let me be. You'll always be there . . .

As he starts to walk over to the bed, another burst of drilling. He stares down at her, transfixed.

Always there . . . The back row of the Continental, and the Mozart, and the maid, and Diana, my Diana . . .

The opening of Mozart's 'Requiem in D Minor' fades in.

Dido . . . Di . . . Di-de-di . . .

He lowers himself onto the bed as the lights fade. The Mozart continues until the lights come up on:

SCENE FOUR

The verandah. DON, *with a carrier bag, staring at* HOWARD *asleep in a wheelchair – he's lost the use of his left side, although his speech remains unimpaired. Silence.* HOWARD *suddenly jerks awake with a startled gasp.*

DON. Sorry, I didn't mean to –

HOWARD. Jesus!

DON. I rang but . . . I knocked too, then –

HOWARD. Jesus!

DON. – I saw that the side gate was open so . . .

HOWARD. Christ . . .

DON. Sorry . . .

Beat.

HOWARD. What the fuck are you doing here?

DON. I was in the vicinity.

HOWARD. Why?

DON. My mother. This is where she wanted her ashes scattered. I come here each anniversary, but somehow I can never bring myself . . .

HOWARD. Your mother?

DON. Yes.

HOWARD. But she died –

DON. Sixteen years ago, I know.

Beat.

How's things?

HOWARD. Never better.

DON. Good.

Beat.

I'm not too bad myself.

HOWARD *watches him warily.*

HOWARD. She's not here.

DON. Who?

HOWARD. Diana.

DON. Out, is she?

HOWARD. Gone.

DON. Gone?

HOWARD *nods.*

Where?

HOWARD. Hornsey. Fell for a bloke in the dock. He got sent down and they married in clink.

DON. What was his crime?

HOWARD. Stealing my wife.

Beat.

Fraud. She obviously had a penchant for cheats.

DON. What are you up to?

HOWARD. Not a lot. You?

DON. UNICEF.

HOWARD. Still footloose? Fancy free?

DON. How's Hermia?

HOWARD. Fine.

DON. Where does she live now?

HOWARD. She's still living here.

DON. Is she in?

HOWARD. No. She's gone to Snakewood. One of those bloody concerts.

DON. Right.

HOWARD. Took up hypnotherapy.

Beat.

They both live here.

DON. Both?

HOWARD. Hermia and Celia.

DON. Who's Celia?

HOWARD. Hermia's girl. Should be back soon.

DON. She's got a daughter?

HOWARD. Yeah. Try and teach them. What's the point? Up the duff at seventeen.

DON. Like Diana, I seem to remember.

HOWARD. You always did. That's your problem. Like a fucking elephant.

Beat.

My little Hermia. Knocked up by a projectionist at the Paradise. Dozy tyke. Still, love is blind.

DON. She loved him?

HOWARD. For about a week.

DON. Well . . . And she was just a girl – when I last saw her.

Beat.

HOWARD. She looks after me. I couldn't do without her – the patience of an angel. I'm quite a handful. I still think of him, y'know, poor Charlie. Can't believe it, even now, dropping dead like that. (*Re. the chair.*) And now this. The heart history in my family . . . Diana's really left us in the shit. Why are you here?

Beat.

DON. I'm not sure. I suppose – suppose I ought to go. Is Hermia . . . ? How is she now?

HOWARD. She's okay.

DON. Good, good. Did she ever . . . ?

HOWARD. What?

DON. Well, she was – all that time ago, she was – in an odd
state, wasn't she?

HOWARD. She's alright.

DON. Good.

HOWARD. Ended as suddenly as it began, just after Charlie's
funeral. Perhaps the shock of his death suddenly hit her –
I don't know – but whatever it was, it all went away. She
never mentioned it again.

DON. Good. That's good.

HOWARD *scrutinises him.*

HOWARD. God, you were an uppity little prat. Got right up
my fucking nose. Every time I saw you, I'd feel my right
hand fisting up. I know I was a bit of a cunt, but, Christ,
I enjoyed it! Still, what's it matter? We're none of us angels,
are we?

DON. I think it does matter.

HOWARD. It was over thirty years ago.

DON. But it still matters. It matters to me. It mattered to my
parents. Of course it matters.

HOWARD. Yeah, well –

DON. It matters that I lost Diana, what we might have been
together, what we might still have been now, and what it's
made me, and how it's left you – and all of us. It matters.
It all matters. Everything does.

HOWARD. Let it go. Move on.

DON. That's all I've ever done.

HOWARD. You're nearly fifty.

DON. Forty-eight.

HOWARD. Look at me, for God's sake! Charlie – thirty-one
when he snuffed it! Don't waste what's left. Blink, and it's
gone. The only useful thing my old man taught me.

Beat.

DON. As men get older, the smell of vanilla increases arousal; for women, it's liquorice and cucumber.

HOWARD *stares at him, bemused.*

What my old man taught me. All the rest of it, all the stuff I've ever learnt, all forgotten.

HOWARD. You know what? You should get out there, find someone, have a kid.

DON *looks at him.*

That'd take you out of yourself.

Beat. DON *picks up his carrier bag.*

(*Re. the bag.*) What have you got in there?

DON. My mother.

In the distance, drifting across from the Heath, we hear the opening of Vivaldi's 'Al Santo Sepolcro'. They look in the direction of the music and listen, then:

I shouldn't be here. It's alright. I won't come again.

CELIA (*off*). Grandad!

Enter CELIA *in a state of excitement. She's thirteen, the spitting image of* HERMIA.

You'll never guess what I've just seen!

She stops in her tracks as she clocks DON. *He stares at her, dumbfounded.*

HOWARD. Hi, honey. This is Don. He used to know Grandma.

DON *continues to stare at her.*

This is Celia.

Beat. DON *smiles at her.*

DON. Hello, Celia.

As he offers her his hand, the lights fade.

End.